Igniting th[

of

Your Creative Mind

YOUR WEALTH IS IN THE POWER OF YOUR CREATIVE
MIND WHICH YOU USE TO ADD VALUE TO PEOPLE

Ferdinard Senyo Lawson

2012

Published by

Ferdinard Senyo Lawson

No. 24 Onyasia Crescent

Roman Ridge

Accra, Ghana

Email: ferdinardl@hotmail.com

Tel: 00 233 0243493859/0244987452

~~0044-7958500337~~/ 0044-7538034723 (UK)

07456521001

ISBN 978 – 9988 –1– 6543 –7

Cover design by Tolu Shofule (tolu@imaginovation.co.uk)

To

The Lord God Almighty

whose creative power and wisdom enabled
me to contribute my knowledge and wisdom to
my generation and generations to come

All Men and Women

who have contributed positively to the world
by unlocking the secrets of the mind, and leaving
us legacies to impact our world through igniting
our individual creative minds

My Family

especially my children, Prince Joshua and Princess
Jessica, who have taught me about the power
of our individual creative mind-set

&

Whoever

I have taught some useful things.

Contents

Acknowledgement

My sincere thanks go to my father of destiny, Rev. Dr. Bishop Michael Hutton-Wood, who himself is a writer and the founder of the House of Judah (Praise) Ministries Worldwide, and has the mandate to raise generational leaders to impact nations by empowering men and women to release their full potential to maximize their destinies.

I express my profound gratitude to Rev. Dr. Paul Yaw Frimpong-Manso (General Superintendent of the General Council of Assemblies of God, Ghana), for his prayers and encouragement that brought this book into reality. May God richly bless you.

Finally, I want to express my sincere gratitude to my spiritual mentor, Pastor Charles Owusu (of Deeper Christian Life Bible Church, Ghana). You are a great inspiration to me and my family, both here in United Kingdom and in Ghana. God bless you.

vi

Introduction

It is very true that the world is actually ruled by people who use their creative mindset to generate things the world has not seen before. By igniting your mindset, you can shape your whole world mentally and transform people's attitude toward life's events. Failures and successes come through the choices we make in life depending on our individual approach and the mind that we have.

Our thoughts influence our existence, just as our environment also depends on how we set our minds to see positive results. In fact, our happiness or unhappiness depends on whether our thoughts are positive or negative. Ultimately, our individual minds predict whether or not we will fulfil our potential and impact nations. It is therefore crucial that we start to ignite the power of our creative mind today, right now, so that we can develop amazing things to add value to our world.

Someone has said, "Our individual mind power is all that's required to create and experience the kind and quality of life that we all desire for ourselves." This world is depending on your creative mind to move forward.

Until we become consciously aware of our creative mind and the power it carries and make a conscious and intentional choice to discover how to utilise the limitless creative power provided us, this world will never appreciate the visions, hopes, dreams and desires that we hold for ourselves. Let the world know that you were here by igniting the power of your creative mind to influence your society positively.

What does it mean to ignite the power of your creative mind? To ignite is to set on fire, to light up or to activate, to arouse or excite a feeling and passion in you.

You cannot do anything without having a force backing you. Therefore, to be able to set on fire or to arouse your creative mind, you need that force (power) to drive you or propel you to actually activate or stimulate your mind to create your desired future. Power is defined as strength, energy, vigour, might and a force at which work is done. That is why you need that force to propel you to activate your mind to create something beneficial to mankind.

Your wealth in life is determined by your creative thinking. It is so interesting to know that once an individual acknowledges the full potential of his thoughts and how much they can transform or change the direction of his life, he will dedicate his full attention to the very thoughts he is thinking. The word of God tells us, "For as he thinketh in his heart, so is he..." (Proverbs 23:7).

In James Allen's book, *As a Man Thinketh*, I discovered that men make or unmake themselves. Allen also discovered that, "In the armoury of thought, a man forges the weapons by which he destroys himself. He also fashions the tools with which he builds for himself heavenly mansions of joy and strength and peace. By the right choice and true application of thought, man ascends to the Divine Perfection."

This teaches us that once we ignite our mind power to its fullest potential, it enables us to develop the personal power that we were created with to create our desired future.

Because of the efficacy and the strength (power) of our mind, Paul the Apostle encourages us to renew our mind (thought) in order to do the acceptable will of God.

> And do not be conformed to this world, but be ye transformed by the renewing of your mind, that you may prove what is that good and acceptable and perfect will of God. (Romans 12:2)

It is necessary also to know that dwelling on a positive and productive mind can produce effective results while negative and fruitless thoughts result in less production. This is to say that, what you sow in your mind, what you ignite or set on fire can only produce its kind. You cannot be thinking of successful keys and how to overcome poverty and be poor in life. Successful thinking can only bring about successful outcomes in your life.

As you read this book, may the Holy Ghost himself empower you to ignite the power of your creative mind to create your desired future. May your life never remain the same. What you think about yourself is exactly what you become. Be empowered in Jesus' name. Amen.

1

The Power of Self-Discovery

The secret of concentration is the secret of self-discovery.
You reach inside yourself to discover your personal
resources, and what it takes to match them to the
challenge. (Arnold Palmer)

Discovering of one-self is actually uncovering or finding your real nature or personality. It can also be termed as "the act or process of achieving self-knowledge."

The power behind knowing ourselves motivates us to appreciate and understand ourselves better and this enables us to make choices and decisions regarding the direction of our lives. It is also the process of being aware of your personal strengths and weaknesses which you adapt and overcome at any given time and situation. This however gives you the full image of yourself that you cannot be like any other person.

Self-discovery enables you to understand the way you actually feel and behave. In fact, it also gives you the platform or opportunity and sets you free into the unknown world to change and create your future. As Bishop Michael

1

Hutton-Wood says, "Without knowing who you are, self-acceptance and change become impossible."

Igniting your creative mind changes your approach to life and your perspective about how, when, what and where to focus your strengths most in order to achieve greater results.

It is true that God Almighty has a master plan for each and every one of us; until we discover that plan by igniting or activating the power of our mind to see that very plan, we cannot actually use it to its full potential. It is our duty or responsibility to engage our minds to see that very purpose of God for our lives.

Discovering of self determines your achievement and assessment in life. That is why it is important that you discover the purpose and assignment that God has for you.

The power of self-discovery enhances your self-esteem and self-assurance (confidence) and more importantly, boosts your morale into success.

I have keenly observed my children and discovered that each one of them is unique and has developed different peculiar qualities. For example, Prince Joshua's good communication skills, assertiveness and emotional control are completely different from Princess Jessica's.

It does not mean that one is better than the other but I have noticed that each one is unique. Therefore discover yourself before you are discovered by somebody else who may start dictating to you what to do in life. This will lead you into frustration because you will be living by their scripts. Having discovered their individual assertiveness through the power of self-discovery, my children now believe in themselves as individuals, respecting their human rights and really demanding what they want differently without fighting each other.

Discovering yourself gives you the platform to achieve something greater in life because knowing yourself affects and influences your self-esteem, personality and well-being. This is to say that lack of knowledge about yourself limits your potential and how much you achieve in life. Just as the Bible makes it clear in Hosea 4:6 that, "My people are destroyed for lack of knowledge."

> *Knowing others is wisdom, knowing yourself is enlightenment.*
>
> LAO TZU

If you don't know that you can achieve a better grade in school, you will never even try to study because you have limited and excluded yourself from success. Knowledge about yourself gives you power to break through barriers and limitations. You actually control your behaviour and deploy your ability to overcome terrible situations simply because you have discovered that you have the ability to stand out in the midst of the crowd at any given time.

The power of self-discovery brings you enlightenment, making you more determined to go all out to work smart to see a particular vision or dream come to pass in your life. I have also discovered that you become very disciplined when you discover yourself. It is through discipline that your character, skills and trade become well-developed for you to take hold of your goals correctly.

"The mind of the prudent acquires knowledge, and the ear of the wise seeks knowledge," says Proverbs 18:15. The power of self-discovery takes away fear of failure and pushes you toward what you can do to overcome that fear that limits you from achieving something productive. You develop a determined mindset that says nothing can stop you except you yourself. Sometimes fear comes to all of us to try and prevent us from stepping out into that needed career, studies, relationship or business. But you need to remain disciplined and focused on that dream for as Henry Ward Beecher says, "A man's true state of power and riches is to be himself."

This is the more reason why you have to stay very alert and cautious in the face of fear and keep moving forward. It is necessary to acknowledge that fear exists but you adapt to it and overcome it so that your precious destiny is not held back. Rather, take positive steps to make productive changes in your life.

It is through the power of self-discovery that you renew your mind about what you carry within you that the world is waiting for. You begin to unlearn some old things and learn new ideas. You cannot expect to influence the world when you have not renewed your mind about certain things that may not be necessary in the 21st Century.

> *Ninety percent of the world's woes come from people not knowing themselves, their abilities, their frailties, and even their real virtues. Most of us go almost all the way through life as complete strangers to ourselves - so how can we know anyone else?*
>
> SIDNEY J. HARRIS

2

Renew Your Mindset

And do not be conformed to this world, but be transformed by the renewing of your mind, that you may prove what is that good and acceptable and perfect will of God. (Romans 12:2)

Until individuals renew and change their minds on negative experiences that limit them, their future is not going to be maximized because as humans, our mind influences our behaviour.

Everything we do is by choice and if you want to see a change in your personal life, then it is necessary that you change the way you view things. Until you are willing to renew your mind daily, minute by minute, practise looking at everything with the word of God concerning your destiny, you will only achieve little because you have not ignited the full power of your mind to create abundance.

Lack of self-discovery and renewal of mindset makes you depressed and can sometimes lead to suicidal thoughts simply because you have become frustrated about life and are not engaging the power of the creative mind to do something profitable with your life.

> *The secret of your future is hidden in your daily routine therefore be careful about what occupies your mind because it will greatly determine what you will become tomorrow.*
>
> BISHOP MICHAEL HUTTON-WOOD

God promises combining a new heart with a brand new mindset to give you the power to be creative or productive in life. You experience an awesome and incredible change in your life and become very successful. This promise can be seen in Ezekiel 36:26-27, "Moreover, I will give you a new heart and put a new Spirit within you; and I will remove the heart of stone from your flesh and give you a heart of flesh. And I will put My Spirit within you."

As we discovered in Chapter One, your mind is the one thing that controls every single action you take to create your destiny. Our mind controls our thoughts. Our mind tells our bodies exactly what to do, create, invest and what not do at any given time of the year.

That is why it is vital that you renew your mindset each day with God's word, against bad memory, depressive feelings, and everything that takes your focus off God.

Attitude determines one's Altitude
The mind is what we use to think. Therefore your life today is the result of what you thought of yesterday. It is very important that you really watch what goes through your mind especially the negative experiences that keep coming

into your mind, and take control of it by renewing it daily.

Bishop Michael Hutton-Wood, has stated in his book, *How to Negotiate your Desired Future with Today's Currency* that the best way to deal with and forget about your negative experiences is to become fruitful and occupy yourself with productive thinking to produce something positive to impact nations.

Renewing your mind with the word of God concerning your destiny gives you assurance which then promotes your confidence in your ability to pursue great things in life. It does not matter your background of failures and shortcomings, when you begin to renew your mindset by changing the way you see yourself then you can embark on the road to achievement.

George Orwell stated in his book, *1984*, "He who controls the past controls the future." In other words, he who ignores the past is condemned to repeat it. So it is necessary that you discipline what goes through your mind (past) so as to be able to move on.

The power of self-discovery makes you see that your birth is not an accident; you are not just born to add to the earth's population. The word of God says that you are a "royal priesthood and a peculiar person", you are born to fill a gap and therefore you are unique. You need to ignite that power of your creative mind to see that you are here to solve the world's problems. You therefore develop your mind through learning and observing the great achievers (role models) in your chosen field of work and education and you follow the same pattern to be great yourself.

I heard Dr. Michael Hutton-Wood once say that, "To

become somebody in particular you have to follow and observe somebody in particular" and that, "Without a role model in your life, you cannot play your role well."

This is to say that creative people learn and observe creative minded people every day to help challenge or ignite the winning spirit that they themselves have.

In the book, *Think like a Winner*, Dr. Walter Staples writes, "The key to success lies in your particular manner of thinking. When you change how you think about yourself, your relationships, your goals, and your world, your life changes. If you change the quality of your thinking, you necessarily will change the quality of your life."

Therefore be very mindful of what you think about and what you allow to control your mind. What you think about surely becomes your character and identity.

If you desire a meaningful and successful life, then you must begin to discover your full potential; renew your mind and engage your creative mind to create something spectacular this world has not seen yet.

Your life today is as a result of what you thought of yesterday. Therefore your happiness depends primarily on your attitude in life, and especially on the nature and quality of your thoughts and ideas, which are more powerful than you may imagine.

Thoughts and ideas are your main weapons in your fight to lead the life you want. You don't see the world as it is, but as your mind sees it. In other words, all your perceptions and thoughts act as a filter between reality and you. The world is what you think it is. If you think it's bad, you won't be able to make progress. Your thoughts influence your existence, as well as your environment. You will be happy or unhappy depending on whether your thoughts are positive or negative.

> *The man who views the world at fifty the same as he did at twenty has wasted thirty years of his life.*
>
> MUHAMMAD ALI

To make your ideas as powerful as possible, they have to be positive. When a negative idea enters your mind, use the sure word of God to get rid of that negative idea and thought. Remember that in life, relationships do not always last forever; therefore it is very important that when people leave your life, you never get angry, bitter or resentful. Just motivate yourself to do better than when they left you. Whatever the case you are more precious to your generation than what people think you are.

Your chosen dream (vision, purpose, and goal) demands the right environment or climate to materialize. It is very vital that you control your environment or the atmosphere around your dream or that atmosphere will definitely control you. This is to say that the individual climate we create knowingly or unknowingly, determines and influences our behaviour and the decisions we make.

It does not matter the negative environment in which you grew up; as long as you are prepared and ready to change that atmosphere with the word of God, you can be assured that you are making progress. As Mike Murdock says, "Nobody else can create your atmosphere for you."

What you see and how you it see controls your mind

and your desire. If you see yourself as great and powerful then you will do the right things to bring those dreams to pass in your life. Therefore do not sit down and wait or hope that somebody else is going to make things happen for you. You have to take control of what goes into your mind. Begin to invest into your future and the environment that inspires you toward excellence and the improvement of your life.

Our thoughts influence our existence, as well as our environment. Your happiness or unhappiness depends on whether your thoughts are ignited positively or negatively Ephesians 4:23 admonishes us to be, "Be renewed in the spirit of your mind." We need to work with our minds by igniting, setting or activating that sense of power not to "Be [...] conformed to this world but be transformed by the renewing of [our] mind."(Romans 12:2)

To "conform" means to assume an outward expression that does not comes from an inward being. In other words, when you conform to something you feel so much influenced that you begin to change the way you act. When you begin to conform to this world system, you are not being faithful to who you really are on the inside. Behind the world system, there is the evil one.

"Transform" means to assume an outward expression that comes from the inward being. This transformation needs to take place in our minds. The Bible cautions us that the carnal mind in itself is enmity against God. The transformation comes from the word of God. When you get the word of God out of the pages of your Bible, read it and ponder over it, then, it gets into your mind and goes down into your spirit. When you keep doing this, you can see your mind lining up with your spirit. This is the key to the transformation. Otherwise, there is this constant battle that goes on between your mind and your spirit.

Strength comes from the trust we have in ourselves
We all are eternal beings. We have an eternal spirit, we live in a mortal body and we have a soul that is made up of the mind, the will and emotions. The only doorway for the enemy into your soul is through your mind. Everything starts with a thought. Before you attempt to do anything, you think about it first. Your mind is the doorway to your deeds. Proverbs 23:7 says, "As a man thinks in his heart, so is he." You cannot have a happy life if you have a sad mind. You need a healthy mind to start with. Our mind is the one that makes us the person God made us to be.

Dr. Charles Stanley once said that, renewing the mind is a little like refinishing furniture. It is a two-stage process involving taking off the old and replacing it with the new. The old is the lies you have learned to tell or were taught by those around you; it is the attitudes and ideas that have become a part of your thinking but do not reflect reality. The new is the truth. To renew your mind is to involve yourself in the

> *No one is more interesting to anybody than that mysterious character we all call "me", which is why self-liberation, self-actualization, self-transcendence, etc., are the most exciting games in town.*
> ROBERT WILSON

process of allowing God to bring to the surface the lies you have mistakenly accepted and replace them with truth. Your desired future lies in your ability to ignite the power of your creative mind.

3

Use Your Talents and Gifts

As every man hath received the gift, even so minister the same one to another, as good stewards of the manifold grace of God. (I Peter 4:10)

By the grace of God each and every individual born by a woman has God-given talent unique to him or her. Therefore we can say that we are gifted or talented in one way or the other. The Bible calls it "ability".

In Acts 11:29, the disciples were given talents and abilities to enable them minister or send relief unto the brethren which were in Judea. Also in Matthew chapter 25:15, we are told that the master having discovered each servant's strength, gift, capability and ability gave them responsibilities, duties or role matching their abilities and went away on his journey.

With self-discovery, we are able to identify the individual talents and abilities God has endowed us with. After you have discovered that talent or gift begin to use it to the glory of God, by adding value to people's lives— then you can say that you are living a fulfilled life.

Having a talent is one thing, discovering it is another, and using that talent is yet another thing altogether. When a person has for example, a gift of singing and never trains to sharpen and develop that gift so as to add value to herself and others, she is neglecting that gift and is likely to lose that beautiful voice. You cannot blame the devil but yourself for losing that talent of singing because you did not identify the need for personal development. In this wise the Preacher strongly counsels that, "Whatsoever thy hand findeth to do, do it with thy might; for there is no work, nor device, nor knowledge, nor wisdom, in the grave, whither thou goest." (Eccles. 9.1)

> *A gift unrecognised and unappreciated is a gift unused.*
> F.S. LAWSON

You cannot say that being gifted as an athlete alone without training is enough to enable you compete against say, Usain Bolt for gold. You cannot be a winner that way.

You have to discover yourself, discover your talent and determine to use that talent maximally before that gift will be recognized and appreciated. Then will you experience the greater opportunities waiting out there for you.

Your life takes shape when you use your talents and gifts. For example your career, family, ministry and your community are improved when you use your God-given talent.

Have you ever thought of how powerful your talent or gift is? Have you sat down and asked yourself questions about how an author becomes a bestseller? How about actors and actresses who have established themselves in their craft? What about those businessmen who are earning millions by doing what they love and what they do best?

My personal story of real writing actually began last year during the summer holiday break from university. Prior to that, I remember that when I was a ten-year old in Ghana, my father always ensured that we had a notebook and a pen anytime we went to church. He demanded that we the children joined him at the adult service. After service, he would ask for, and inspect whatever each of us had written down during church service. The quantity of food that we were served was determined by how well we had written. I know this will sound funny but I think that was one of the best ways to reward us according to our ability to put sentences together and improve our spelling. In fact, at that time I thought it was a punishment but I have come to realize that my father had discovered the talent of writing in us and had been helping us to develop that skill.

In my second year at secondary school, I was regarded as one of the best during our handwriting and spelling contest. I then developed interest in writing my own spiritual tracts to give to people. During evangelism, I made posters from pictures of flowers and trees but never knew I was destined to be a writer.

In 2011, I was due to submit an essay to the university which I showed to a Christian brother who is a teacher and an editor for proof reading. He asked me, "Brother Ferdinand, the way you have presented your essay, have you thought of writing a book?"

Because I had not discovered that I could improve upon

my writing skills and aim at presenting my biblical knowledge through books to add value to mankind, I laughed and said to him, "I cannot write a book." The brother encouraged me to give it a try and see how it would turn out. Incredibly, and by the grace of God, this is my third book since that first step in writing a book. The Bible says that "for lack of knowledge my people are destroyed."

What have you been told that you are capable of doing that you are shying away from? That could be the turning point in your life as you identify that particular thing. By adding value and skill to it and using it to the benefit of

> *Your distress about life might mean you have been living for the wrong reason, not that you have no reason for living.*
> TOM O'CONNOR

others, your life will change for the better. Your talent that you used to add value to the nation brings you before great men and kings as testified in Proverbs 22:29, "Seest thou a man diligent in his business? He shall stand before kings; He shall not stand before mean men."

Dorcas used her talent of sewing to add value to the men and women of her time. Peter also used his fishing talent or skill to impact Jesus' ministry; he became the fisher of men. Ruth was busy working in the field and found her husband Boaz, a rich man of his time.

From today as you uncover or discover your hidden talent and gift and use it to add value to your generations, may God empower you to stand out and shine wherever you are supposed to be great in Jesus name. AMEN.

4
_____

Have a Purpose for Your Life

Where there is no vision, the people perish, but he that keepeth the law, happy is he.   (Proverbs 29: 18)

God always wants a family relationship with you as he is your father. God has a purpose and a plan for our lives; we learn from Hebrews 10:7 that we are created for a specific purpose and as we identify that purpose and plan for our lives, we will begin to have a meaningful and successful life.

However, there is a need to have a plan by actually sitting ourselves down and undertaking careful assessment of our needs and counting the cost involved in fulfilling our dreams. Having a dream, plan or vision alone is not enough, but the counting of the cost of what it may take to realise the dream, plan or vision — "For which of you willing to build a tower, doth not first, having sat down, count the expense, whether he has the things for completing." (Young's Literal Translation)

What does it mean to have a vision for life? The general conception is that the word "vision" has a variety of

17

meanings. It is defined by some as having a purpose, goal or dream. To others, however, there is a clear distinction between vision and purpose.

This chapter focuses on vision (purpose) as the vehicle to drive home what we really can achieve. Having a vision or purpose for your life actually means being determined or persuaded to do or achieve a goal or a dream or to achieve something positive through definitive decision making.

> Daniel purposed in his heart that he would not defile himself with the portion of the king's meat nor with the wine which he drank, therefore he requested the prince of the eunuchs that he might not defile himself. (Daniel 1:8)

Your provision, protection and promotion lie in your purpose which you discover through igniting your creative mind. Having a purpose demands that you keep your eyes fixed exclusively on the dream or goal. You will need to focus absolutely on that purpose, disregarding any distractions wherever they may be coming from.

You will require extreme devotion, commitment and determination to realize the dream or goal. Can you imagine what can happen when a footballer who has placed the ball at the spot kick and waiting for the referee to whistle to take a penalty, decides to look aside while taking the penalty shot, or the driver who while reversing in the corner, fixes his attention or eyes on the sandwich box by his side, rather than concentrating on ensuring safe driving?

A purposeful person is the one who defies all odds and stands by the truth. He buys the truth but will not sell it.

She is that individual who makes up her mind with focus, without allowing any wind of change to distract her.

The ability to succeed in any endeavour in life and to develop the capacity to impact positively on others is dependent on self-denial, sacrifice and commitment as evidenced in in the book of Daniel. Clearly Daniel's purpose was not to defile himself with the king's meat as he knew what the consequences could be.

It is important to have focus, a focus on the goal(s) of our dreams. The journey could be rugged, the paths filled with thorns, disappointments and various challenges, but you must not despair and lose the plot. Hold firm and strong with a great faith like that of the proverbial mustard seed and remain focused on your dream or goal and soon victory will be in sight in God's own time.

We read in II Corinthians 4:18 that, "... we look not at the things which are seen but at the things which are not seen for the things which are seen are temporal, but the things which are not seen are eternal."

When you are not moved or perturbed by the distractions, challenges and discouragements of loved ones and the devil's tricks to abort your dream by taking your eyes off your target, you will appreciate with time, that these hold ups are nothing compared to the fulfilment of a dream.

As we make up your minds to be in fellowship with our heavenly Father, accepting His beloved Son Jesus as our personal Saviour, who died on the cross to save us, holding on to His promises through His word, *nothing* and I mean *nothing* should separate us from this relationship.

Be encouraged in the Lord just as Daniel was. Habakkuk 2: 1-3 reads:

> I will stand upon my watch and set me upon the tower, and will watch to see what he will say unto me, and what I shall answer when I am reproved. And the Lord answered me, and said, write the vision and make it plain upon tables that he may run that readeth it. For the vision is yet for an appointed time, but at the end it shall speak and not lie, though it tarry, wait for it, because it will surely come, it will not tarry.

There is the need to watch and pray concerning your purpose, goal or dream, ensuring your spirit man is driven daily, as there is the tendency to lose focus. Protect and guard your purpose because a number of people out there may not be happy about the achievement of your dream of obtaining good grades at the university, winning that new contract for your business, or finding a life partner and the impending marriage, buying that new car or new home, given the truth of the presence of some pharaohs in our midst at this time desperate to kill that baby of a dream.

In the book of Genesis, Joseph is portrayed as a dreamer. The events that resulted in his being sold into slavery by his brothers, defying Potiphar's wife, interpreting Pharaoh's dreams and finally becoming a prime minister in Egypt, undoubtedly is the clearest testimony of the need to protect and guard our dreams.

Whatever your dream about your future may be, please share it only with your spiritual father, your heavenly Father's appointed representative, who will pray with you, encourage you and stand with you to see that dream come to pass in Jesus' name, Amen.

To make your dreams and desires come true and have the life you really want, you need to form a clear vision of what it is you are after. Then, you need to connect to the word of God to see what God has said concerning that dream. No matter what your desires are, the Almighty God is able to see you through and He can help make them a reality in your life.

Every day, generate positive thoughts that will increase your self-confidence, and nourish your hopes for a better future. Try to let only positive thoughts enter your mind. When you think something negative, let it pass, and focus on the positive. If you do this every day, and if you don't forget to be thankful for the help Almighty God gives you, all your wishes will be granted.

Above all, be patient. Everything happens at its designated time, so be humble and wait patiently for your wish to come true. Wait upon the Lord for He will make His grace available to you when you faint not. Nevertheless, if you have for any reason shared your dreams with people around you for which you may seem to be suffering today, do not be discouraged, do not throw in the towel, keep the faith in our God, for in Him we trust that hope will abound.

He alone is your shield and buckler, your protector who will stand with you and defend your course at all times, who in the process of time will definitely manifest his presence in your life, bringing victory to your doorstep.

In pursuit of your purpose or dream, it is important that you identify your personal strengths and weaknesses. This is the surest way of discovering the necessary steps you need to improve upon yourself in order to achieve your dream. There is no chance of realising a dream when you fail to plan and identify the processes involved in reaching that dream. Many people have failed in life not necessarily due to any interference or limitations imposed on them by any perceived circumstances or the enemy, but clearly due to their own lack of relevant and appropriate knowledge, which of course is the power to success. God says, "My people are destroyed for the lack of knowledge, because thou hast rejected knowledge." (Hosea 4:6)

> *Life without a purpose is life without meaning and the greatest tragedy in life is not death, but life without purpose.*
>
> DR. MYLES MUNROE

Solomon needed wisdom in pursuing his vision, goal and purpose in life as a king, so he asked God, "Give me now wisdom and knowledge that I may go out and come in before this people, for who can judge this thy people that is so great?"(2 Chronicles: 1-10) He knew that without knowledge and a discerning heart to govern God's people, he would not be able to distinguish between right and wrong.

My Bishop once said that, "The future is secured by those who know how to sharpen, use their gifts and their strength by identifying and making the most of the given opportunities."

Patiently waiting on the Lord is necessary. However it is equally important that we rely on informed knowledge to initiate the steps necessary to achieve the heights of life. As David Oyedepo Jnr. puts it, "Your value of knowledge determines your upliftment in life."

Decisiveness of purpose is characterised by firmness and determination to achieve a dream or goal. However, as believers we need to appreciate and understand that decisiveness does not mean being stubborn, arrogant or hasty, but rather being able to decide with speed and clarity of purpose in all matters.

Ruth made a conscious decision to follow her mother-in-law, regardless of any price she might have had to pay. Her determination, conviction, faith, commitment, humility, love, trust, self-belief and above all self-confidence as regards her purpose or goal are no doubt a worthy example.

> And Ruth said, entreat me not to leave thee, or to return from following after thee, for whither thou goest, I will go; and where thou lodgest, I will lodge; thy people shall be my people and thy God my God. Where thou diest, will I die and there will I be buried, the Lord do so to me, and more also if ought but death part thee and me. (Ruth 1: 16-17; Psalm 12: 7-8)

Samuel is also another personality in the Bible who is depicted as a man of courage, faith, conviction and steadfastness in achieving his life's purpose. (1 Samuel 2: 26), so also was Jeremiah who stood firm, and remained focused with faith in his purpose of preaching the word of God, in the midst of his personal tribulations and trials.

The moral lesson I guess is the stark reminder for children of God to develop the capacity for endurance, patience, self-sacrifice and focus which is demonstrated by these personalities. This is very crucial if we are to achieve the dreams and plans God has for us, for without a decision no progress can be made; a meaningless life is worse than cancer.

The word of God cannot lie, whatever He has promised concerning your destiny He will fulfil and cause it to come to pass in your life. In every believer's hands lies the seed of failure or success. Your

> *Everything in the universe has a purpose. Indeed, the invisible intelligence that flows through everything in a purposeful fashion is also flowing through you.*
> WAYNE DYER

decision regarding your purpose will only be achieved depending on your personal decisiveness towards that purpose. Be decisive and let focus be your stock-in-trade, and as I always say, be like a postage stamp on a letter to your destination.

It is my personal opinion that success as well as failure is by choice. All great men and successful persons make some choices at one time or another, a choice which either promotes or collapses their business or enterprise.

In the pursuit of our individual dreams there will be the occasion to make choices and the type of choice we make will determine our success or failure, thus we need to be resolute and focused on our goals and ensure we make the best of all choices, without which we miss the plan our God has purposed for us as his children.

> Trust in the lord with all thine heart; and lean not unto thine own understanding. In all thy ways acknowledge him, and he shall direct thy paths. (Proverbs 3:5-6)

Until we become obsessed with our purpose of life, we cannot be successful; see Joshua 1:8. For it is when all our attention, time and total efforts are given to our dreams, goals and visions that we can experience God's undeserved favour.

Intimidation and bullying can be some of the methods or strategies the enemy may employ to distract us from focusing on our purposes of life.

Let us be like the three Hebrew boys—Shadrach, Meshach and Abednego—who made determined choices and remained focused on their choice of serving only the true and living God, regardless of the intimidation.

Discover yourself; ignite your creative mind and use your God-given talent to create your desired future. Begin to have a purposeful life.

5

Avoid Dream-Killers

Come now, let's kill him and throw him into one of these cisterns and say that a ferocious animal devoured him. Then we'll see what comes of his dreams.

(Genesis 37:20)

We discover in the life of Joseph that his own brothers' plan and motive was to stop the birth of his dream and his purpose. They did not care if they had to kill him with the dream. One thing is sure – those dream killers may try to kill the dreamer but not the dream. Dream killers are determined to stop the birth of our vision at whatever cost, so scripture advises us:

> Now I beseech you, brethren, mark them which cause divisions and offences contrary to the doctrine which ye have learned; and avoid them. For they that are such serve not our Lord Jesus Christ, but their own belly; and by good words and fair speeches deceive the hearts of the simple. (Romans 16:17-18)

To avoid them means to turn away from, to turn aside, turning away from those who cause offences and occasions of stumbling, turning away from dream killers, division mongers and those who deliberately cause pain and havoc to your destiny. It means that we are to keep out of their way and not to fall in with them. Avoid them; have nothing to do with them. When it comes to your purposes in life, you need to actually look out for those people who may discourage you from your assignment in life and avoid them completely. Follow the advice in Proverbs 12:26, "A righteous person is cautious with friendship, but the way of the wicked leads them astray."

It is sometimes said that our countenance is always determined by the people we call loved ones and friends. They either add to us or subtract from us, making or breaking us into such pieces beyond repair. No doubt men of wisdom are very careful about the type of people they associate with. No association leaves us neutral. In Psalm 1:1, we are admonished not to even walk with evil people.

> Blessed is the man that walketh not in the counsel of the ungodly, nor standeth in the way of sinners, nor sitteth in the seat of the scornful.

> *People in our lives are like buttons in an elevator which take us up to the top floor, keep us on the ground or to the basement.*
> BISHOP MICHAEL HUTTON-WOOD

In the pursuit of our individual plans and purposes, we must avoid the company of those people who do not in any way share our vision or have our interest at heart. Many a time, others may try discouraging us if we allow them to do so. We must heed the advice to learn to listen to God and let his word dwell in us richly. We should make a conscious effort and decision to ignore discouragers by avoiding them as much as possible as they are never part of God's promises to us. The Bible encourages us in Proverbs 1:15, 'My son, do not go along with them, do not set foot on their paths.'

God has a purpose, a plan for you, a bright and great future and you must not allow negative people to sow seeds of discouragement in your life and distract you from the great dream and vision of God's divine purpose.

> Oh, the joys of those who do not follow the advice of the wicked, or stand around with sinners, or join in with mockers. (Psalm1:1)

There are examples of Bible characters who were faced with discouragement, but encouraged themselves and rose above the discouragement. They made up their minds to focus on and pursue their dreams — David (Psalm 55:5-6); Elijah (1 Kings 19:4); Hannah (1 Samuel 1)

Do not be discouraged by either the action or reaction of other people, rather use their actions towards you to develop and build a mindset of progress and prosperity.

We may come face to face with challenges and attacks, but remember the word of God encourages us to be unmovable and unshakeable on these occasions. We are empowered by God's purpose and plan for our lives, as his word is always true and it will come to pass in our lives.

Be consoled that no successful and forward moving person goes through life without occasional episodes of discouragement. What is relevant and important is the development of an appropriate attitude to the problem so as to withstand and overcome it.

In this way only one thing is certain, victory in the name of the almighty God. Strangely, sometimes following this divine victory, the enemy becomes jealous and envious of the manifestation of God's presence in our lives as evidenced in the biblical accounts regarding Hannah, when the Lord answered her prayers for a son.

You may be discouraged because of unfulfilled desires and dreams in your life—your marriage is delaying; your strong desire of becoming a mother is not being fulfilled; your finding it difficult to pass your exams etc.

Financial difficulties can cause great pain, anxiety and discouragement to many people. When faced with financial challenges, you may have to sow financial seeds in faith, to trigger financial breakthrough in your own family life.

Do not be discouraged, our God is a prayer answering God, a God of fulfilled promises. Wait upon him and it is just a matter of time before your desires come to fruition in Jesus' name.

Mary and Martha experienced discouragement, and we are told it was out of a feeling of disappointment at the Lord Jesus' lateness over the death of their brother Lazarus; "If you had been here, my brother would not have died," Martha said in John 11:21.

Peter experienced discouragement because of his personal failure. Having denied the Lord three times, he went out and wept bitterly, perhaps because he felt he had really blown it for good. How could he deny the Lord, the one he promised never to deny?

Reflecting on my personal life, I can identify with Peter's feelings of inadequacy; how often I have failed, and repeated the same old mistakes of life. When I realised my mistake I would get frustrated and discouraged and feel that I have let myself down. Such moments were sad times and I thought I was never going to make it in life, but thank God for my Bishop. His words of counselling and encouragement uplifted and motivated me to return to the university where I am currently undertaking degree studies in Public Health and Social Care.

I have been a student's representative in my university for two consecutive years. I can assure you that our God is not only a God of second chances, but also a God of fresh starts, of new beginnings. Do not be discouraged if your plans do not succeed for the first time.

Never give up on yourself but hold steadfastly unto God's word for your life. You are not born to lose but born to win as reggae star Jimmy Cliff sings, "I am born to win."

> *No one learns to walk by taking only one step.*
> CATHERINE PULSIFER

Remember also that delay is not denial. Once you discover yourself and your purpose in life, you will understand how true it is that most people overestimate what they can accomplish in a year.

Nobody is immune to discouragement. Our Lord Jesus Christ himself faced discouragement when the people failed him due to ignorance and lack of understanding during his ministry. At times, you may have genuine reasons for sharing your dreams or visions with some other people, who may be disinterested in whatever you may be sharing with them and therefore may dismiss you with scorn and disdain. Do not be bothered or discouraged about this attitude, stand firm in the Lord and hold on to your dream,

> These things I have spoken unto you, that in me ye might have peace. In the world ye shall have tribulation, but be of good cheer; I have overcome the world. (John 16:33)

Avoid dream-killers

John 16:33 discloses that discouragement is part of every believer's journey; it is a normal and unavoidable emotion we have to deal with. That scripture enjoins us to take heart in times of challenges or discouragements, something that is reinforced in Romans 16:17 and Titus 3:10 —

> Now I beseech you brethren, mark them which cause divisions and offences contrary to the doctrine which ye have learned, and avoid them.

> Warn a divisive person once, and then warn him a second time. After that, have nothing to do with him.

Identify the dream-killers

David demonstrated openness and honesty in placing his concerns before the Lord. (1 Samuel 30:1-6) David begins to defeat his discouragement by identifying it. We need to bring our discouragements in the open so that we are able to seek the face of the Lord in confronting and or dealing with them just as David did.

Identify the people around you who may have the penchant for discouraging you, avoid them as much as possible and focus on the word of the Lord and His promises for you. The account of Jarius' daughter and Jesus' assurance to her father is evidence of the necessity of avoiding or ignore elements of discouragement around us.

Be encouraged in yourself

We must believe in ourselves or no one else will believe in us. The Bible said David encouraged himself in the Lord, he kept reminding himself of who God is and who his children are. (1 Samuel 30:6)

> *We must match our aspirations with the competence, courage and determination to succeed.*
>
> ROSALYN SUSSMAN YALOW, A US MEDICAL PHYSICST

David was discouraged because of an enemy who was jealous of him and trying to destroy him. Do you have some people in your life who are consciously trying to do you harm?

Are there some people close to you who are jealous or mean or vindictive? That can be very discouraging.

Oh, that I had wings of a dove'! David wrote; 'I would fly away and be at rest, I would hurry to my place of shelter, far from the tempest and storm. (Psalm 55:5-6)

What do you say to yourself when you are discouraged? Do you speak more discouraging words to yourself? Learn to give a sacrifice of praise unto the Lord and worship him with thanksgiving, and as time goes on, the heavenly father who gives good gifts to his children will definitely show up in the midst of your circumstances.

Use your talent in God's house

One other way of addressing your own discouragement is to motivate others. Proverbs 11:25, "He who refreshes others will himself to be refreshed." Instead of looking for someone to pick you up, look around to see who *you* can pick up. Thank goodness, we can be motivators even when we feel discouraged and in the process of time you may become a motivator and lessen yours.

> Not forsaking the assembling of ourselves together, as the manner of some is; but exhorting one another; and so much the more, as ye see the day approaching. (Hebrew 10:25)

One good cure for discouragement is to simply get involved in church activities. Find a department within your church and be committed and loyal to offering your services. This may encourage you and change your mood. At times when we are discouraged, we become frustrated, unmotivated and feel betrayed. But as you join forces with other believers to undertake God's work, you will become motivated and encouraged, and of course be uplifted, thereby overcoming fear and anxiety. Spend some time in the fellowship of those people with strong faith, share the word of God and meditate on the word. We need to get together more often, even in the midst of our busy lives, because we need each other to stay encouraged.

Encouragement is one of the most important things we all need and expect when we are discouraged or downhearted. That is why in Jude 1:19-21, the Bible says,

> But you, beloved, building yourselves up on your most holy faith, praying in the Holy Spirit, keep yourselves in the love of God, looking for the mercy of our Lord Jesus Christ unto eternal life.

We need positive and productive people in our lives to motivate us to keep pressing on in the faith, to build us up in the Christian journey so that we do not lose hope but stay on course and stay alert. It takes self-discipline and self-motivation to bring us close to God. Therefore, it is very important that we know the word. Galatians 6:1 educates us that,

> Brethren, if a man is overtaken in any trespass, you who are spiritual restore such a one in a spirit of gentleness, considering yourself lest you also be tempted.

This is to say that trying to stand alone without a good fellowship with other Christian brethren can bring you face to face with discouragement.

Dwell on God's word daily

Romans 15:4 informs us that everything that was written in the past was written to teach us, so that through endurance and the encouragement of the scriptures we might have hope. Train yourself get into the word of God even if it seems dry and lifeless to you, keep reading and you will be encouraged and uplifted.

> Let the word of Christ dwell in you richly in all wisdom; teaching and admonishing one another in psalms and hymns and spiritual songs, singing with grace in your hearts to the Lord (Colossians 3:16)

When we allow God's word to dwell in our lives, it changes and transforms us to have God's very nature. It also becomes treasured in our lives.

> All scripture is given by inspiration of God, and is profitable for doctrine, for reproof, for correction, for instruction in righteousness, that the man of God may be complete, thoroughly equipped for every good work. (2 Timothy 3:16)

Furthermore, the word of God allows us to drop off all negative things that disturbed us at one time, and in many cases, overcame us. Amazingly, the word of God makes you healthy in your physical appearance with the glory of the Lord shinning in your face. Meditating on God's word creates calmness in your spirit and even eliminates or reduces the symptoms of many illnesses.

> Do not let this Book of the Law depart from your mouth; meditate on it day and night, so that you may be careful to do everything written in it. Then you will be prosperous and successful. (Joshua 1:8, NIV)

Bible characters who avoided dream-killers

Elijah – Elijah was discouraged because of exhaustion. After a great spiritual victory, when he called down fire from heaven and destroyed all the prophets of Baal, one woman scared him to death because she threatened to kill him. And he was ready to give up. He said, "I have had enough, Lord, he said. Take my life; I am no better than my ancestors." (1 Kings 19:4)

I find that I am often discouraged after spiritual

victories. How about you? Do you often find yourself discouraged just when God has done something wonderful in your life? It's not unusual.

Hannah – Hannah was discouraged because the deepest desire of her heart had not been given to her. And it was a good and worthy desire—to have a baby that she could give back to the Lord. Downhearted and discouraged, in bitterness of soul, Hannah wept very much and prayed to the Lord for a baby. (1 Sam.1)

You may be discouraged because of unfulfilled desires. Maybe it's the desire to be married, but the right person hasn't come along. Maybe, like Hannah, it's the desire to have a baby, but your womb has been closed so far. Maybe it's your dream of serving God in some special way, but the door hasn't opened yet. Unfulfilled desires can be discouraging. We can certainly see that discouragement is nothing new; it's been around since the beginning of time.

Naomi – Naomi was discouraged because of financial difficulties and terrible loss. Her husband and two sons had both died, and she was left penniless and homeless. "Don't call me Naomi," she told her friends. "Call me Mara (meaning bitter), because the Almighty has made my life very bitter..." (Ruth 1:20-21). It's easy enough to understand her discouragement. Financial difficulties cause a great deal of discouragement for many of us.

Mary and Martha — Mary and Martha were discouraged because they lost someone they loved; they had really expected Jesus to save him. After all, Jesus had been healing other people of all kinds of diseases, surely, he would come and save his beloved friend, Lazarus, they reasoned. And when he didn't, they were very discouraged; Jesus had disappointed them. "Lord," Martha said to Jesus, "if you had been here, my brother would not have died." (John 11:21). Have you ever set an agenda for the Lord, expecting him to work on your timetable, and then been disappointed when he didn't come through? That can be discouraging.

Peter — Peter was discouraged because of his own failure. After he denied the Lord three times, he went out and wept bitterly. I imagine he felt that he had blown it for good, and he must have been terribly discouraged with himself. How could he deny the Lord, the One he promised never to deny? When I look at myself and see how inadequate I am, how often I fail, how I go back and do the same things over and over that I know I shouldn't do, I get very discouraged. In fact, that discourages me probably more than anything else. How about you?

Jesus — Even Jesus fought discouragement when his friends failed him; when he was misunderstood; when he tried to help and his help was refused. That really hurts, when you have totally good motives, and yet people don't approve understand or support you. In fact, they may reject you, as they did Jesus.

It is encouraging to see that even these great people of God went through times of discouragement. God understands discouragement; discouragement is a normal and unavoidable emotion that we must all deal with. It comes to us in different ways, for different reasons, and at different times, but rest assured that the grace of God is sufficient for us in times of discouragement and He will surely see us through if we faint not.

> And he said unto me, my grace is sufficient for thee: for my strength is made perfect in weakness. Most gladly therefore will I rather glory in my infirmities, that the power of Christ may rest upon me. (II Corinthians 12:9)

6

You are Above all Limits

Do not rejoice over me, O my enemy. Though I fall I will rise; though I dwell in darkness, the LORD is a light for me. (Micah 7:8)

Limitations are any form of rules, situations and circumstances that prevent free movement. It may also be any form of condition that limits an individual's ability to improve, due to a defect, a failing and, or a short-coming. Limitations may come in many forms— some may be imposed by others, some by misconceptions, while others may be self-imposed.

Limitations may sometimes exist purely because of our own individual perspectives about life's circumstances. Nevertheless, as Christians, the way we view our perceived limitations and those of others can affect the way and manner we may deal with them. It is very important however that our response must be through the word of God. We may not always be able to control the limitations that confront us in our daily lives, but the possibility is that we can achieve this feat through the powerful word of God.

We may be born with some limitations, while we may acquire some along life's journey. Jabez was labelled as "sorrow" at birth because his mother gave birth to him in pain. (1 Chronicles 4: 9-11) Here sorrow and pain were the main limitations to achieving victory or success.

Maybe your life has been associated with painful and sorrowful events, and as you grow older, negative things are being said about you. Your peers may be calling you names which may be associated with your family history. Some family members may have rejected you because your birth was not what they actually expected.

At times we may suffer certain things or go through certain experiences or challenges of life, not because we originate them but perhaps because of our connection to certain family backgrounds and therefore suffer various degrees of labelling with negativities, and may even be spoken against and called derogatory names. You may also suffer the experience of being told in the face you will not succeed in any life pursuits or endeavours. These experiences could limit your progress; but as you discover yourself, renew your mind and begin to use your talent and gift, you will be celebrated. What have you been called? This could be the limiting factor to your progress in life.

> O that thou wouldest bless me indeed, and enlarge my coast, and that thine hand might be with me, and that thou wouldest keep me from evil, that it may not grieve me. (1 Chronicle 4: 10)

This is the proverbial Prayer of Jabez. He knew that things were not going on well with him and for him to make any progress in his life, things had to change. Jabez did not allow the history of his birth to limit him in any way and therefore resorted to fellowship and communion with God through the power of prayer. He never focused on the labels and ridicules of his contemporaries, but called upon his God the almighty as David did when confronted with the challenges of Goliath the Philistine.

My opinion is that Jabez may have read Psalm 27:10 — "When my father and mother forsake me, the Lord will look after me." Perhaps he saw beyond his limitation and the labels, and discovered that he had something the world was looking for. Until he discovered those talents, and the blessing of God on his life, he was going nowhere in life.

So he called on God the giver of life, purpose, dreams, gifts and talents to answer him speedily. And the God who has said, "Call unto me and 1 will answer you, and show you great and mighty things..." (Jeremiah 33: 3), answered him.

Evidently, no matter the negative opinions and notions that others may hold against you, as you desire change, using the small gift or talent to influence the people around, you will see that change in the name of Jesus.

As we grow and mature in life, it is our responsibility to change the very things we dislike or are uncomfortable with. There is no doubt in my mind that my parents did their best for me as a child. But with the progress of time I have come to the realization that I can make certain changes in my personal life, given my strong belief now that one has the choice and the responsibility to make those changes necessary regarding how one turns up in life. It is a decision that may change our lives and destinies and impact positively on generations to come.

Therefore until we become restless and obsessed with our present circumstances, we cannot make any changes that may impact positively on the lives of others.

Jabez discovered that his family background was different from that of his peers. He understood and appreciated the exigency of paying a price through prayer to effect the needed change in his personal lifestyle. Surely, Jabez may have come to terms with the hard truth that for him to experience a better life, he had to renew his mind-set about himself.

> *The future is what you make it and not what you think it should be, but is created by those who turn adversity into advantage and do not allow their past to hold their life hostage.*
>
> BISHOP MICHAEL HUTTON-WOOD

Remember that you are the prophet of your own destiny and it is when you have discovered yourself and begun to take steps of faith and developed the right mind-set and positive attitude to effect change in your personal life that life becomes meaningful.

Jabez was requesting that the God of Israel should empower him to maximize his destiny so as to bring joy and glory to God. He also acknowledged the fact that some limitations have been placed on his destiny and that to break through, God will have to extend his boundaries and surroundings which can enable him to take over and not take cover.

You may have been limited in areas of business or career

perhaps due to financial constraints. You may have requested the heavenly father to give you wisdom, understanding, patience, humility, love and joy within your specific spheres of life endeavours or made a request for divine health so as to stay in perfect health. Know that God says, "I wish above all things that thou be in good health and prosper..."(3 John 1:2)

It is God's desire that His children prosper so as to bless others instead of limiting the prosperity to ourselves. God told Abraham, "I will make you a great nation, and I will bless you, and make your name great; and so you shall be a blessing." (Genesis 12: 2-3)

Another lesson here is that Jabez knew he could reach far and accomplish more in life so as to have a more positive impact. His perception was that God is able to do exceedingly, abundantly above all that we ask or think, according to the power that works in us (Ephesians 3: 20)

Although Jabez was limited, he knew that God is unlimited, reminding us that we cannot think the same as God, as His ways are not our ways and are above our ways. His thoughts are above our thoughts. His love we can grow in, but never grasp fully. He desires to fill us with his fullness and to get us out of the way of limitations and failures, as it is not His wish that these shortcomings become our portion. God's unlimited blessings are also reflected in 2 Kings 4:6

> And it came to pass, when the vessels were full, that she said unto her son, bring me another vessel. And he said unto her, there is not a vessel more, and the oil ceased.' So long as there were vessels to be filled, the miraculous flow

of oil continued and it only ceased when there were no more jars to contain it.

The lady had just enough vessels to contain the flow of oil, thus she had limited numbers of vessels when God had unlimited flow of oil of blessings to change her life and that of her entire generation. From the account, she had the opportunity to go and borrow extra vessels but made the choice to limit the prophet who did not speak any word to stop the flow of the oil. This is to say that our readiness to allow God to expand our limited ideas, vessels, nets and indeed our coast in making impact can only be made possible if we stop limiting the power of God.

George Washington, the first President of the USA, had problem with reading and writing but never allowed his limitation to take hold of his destiny.

Steven Spielberg, the movie maker also struggled with math and dropped out of high school.

Actor Tom Cruise's childhood was extremely lonely. He was dyslexic and lots of kids made fun of him but he was determined not to allow his disability to stop him from using his talents and gifts. He rather used those experiences to create his desired future by learning to accept ridicule.

Reyn Geyer the inventor of Nerf balls & Twister was also dyslexic but he was very determined to overcome his disability. He ignited the power of his creative mind to discover his talents and develop products to help others who struggled through school as he did.

Michael Faraday became one of the greatest in his days even though the resources he had at that time, as a blacksmith were limited. However he did rise above his limitation and became one of the world's greatest discoverers in the area of science and humanity.

Henry Ward Beecher's childhood days were very bad. Sometimes due to his lack of effective communication in the area of writing and spelling, he was regarded as foolish and stupid. Through his self-discovery he also saw above the limitations that were placed on him (foolish and stupid) and became a prominent Congregationalist, social reformer, abolitionist and a great speaker.

What have you been called? It does not matter what they call you, as long as you will discover yourself in God's word (the manual for living) designed for your good, and your accomplishment in life, and you will be above those limitations.

It did not matter to all these people listed above, what they have been labeled with. Regardless of their individual shortcomings, bad academic records, etc., they bounced back and rose above all limits by igniting the power of their creative mind to create something spectacular in life. Some became powerful scientists, lawyers, doctors, politicians etc. This is your season and your turn to ignite your creative mind to change your world. No limitation is above God and we should not fail in life, because no amount of limitation under the universe can restrain the blessings of God in our lives.

Bishop Hutton-Wood has said that, "When purpose is unknown; abuse is inevitable." For example, if you do not know the purpose of a television set, there is the tendency for you to want to use it as a side table and place a bottle of

Coca-Cola on it or even want to break the glass and use it as a money safe. It sounds funny yes, and it may be indeed, and you may be as described in Hosea 4:6. "For lack of knowledge my people are destroyed."

At times believers pray for miracles and blessings for their lives without taking the time to find out the purpose of their requests. There are always reasons for miracles and blessings that come into our lives. It is very important that we do not allow our miracles and blessings to become a stumbling block between us and our good Lord who makes these provisions abundantly available to us. He told Abraham, "I will bless you and ye shall be a blessing to mankind."

Whatever we desire of God, let us remember that it would be within a progress of time, within which God may be testing our ability to manage the miracles and the blessings that, that job, child, promotion etc. will bring. It is important that we do not allow such manifestations of the Lord's fulfilment of his promises to take away his glory. When this happens we cause much pain to our almighty God and as Isaiah 42:8 succinctly puts it, "God's glory will not be shared with any man."

It is in this view that Jabez prayed not to fall into temptation and that evil people should not harm him. (Something which happens to many successful people). It is significant to note the aspect of Jabez's prayer where he asks for protection from harm and pain.

7

Don't Give Up on Yourself

But the path of the just is as the shining light, that shineth more and more unto the perfect day.
(Proverbs 1:18)

In the early stages of pregnancy a baby is likely to be lost. This also applies to our God-given dream; therefore we need to protect it and ensure it is preserved. The enemy tried so hard to destroy Moses and Jesus before they reached their second birthday. The question is why? Simply because the enemy feared their future and he fears your future too.

In addition, when a prospective mother is pregnant, she has to do certain things in order to deliver what God has promised her. Therefore you may ask why some pregnant women still drink alcohol, smoke and eat certain types of food and you cannot do the same? The answer is that what you are carrying is different from what they are carrying. Your dream is different from theirs.

Remember that, pursuing your dream requires daring to be different, even some may be radical changes but you have to do it to see your dream come true. (Isaiah 52:1;

47

Eph. 5:14; 1 Samuel 30:1-8) Sometimes it will demand that you disconnect from some relationship and habits that can hurt you. It will also require you to stay out of certain places and re-order

> *The future is created by those who don't have everyone as a friend.*
>
> BISHOP MICHAEL HUTTON-WOOD

your priorities according to your God-given destiny, not popular consent.

Esther's vision meant that she decided to put her life on the line and say, "If perish, I perish." She did not even perish even though she was willing to die for her vision.

It is sometimes shocking to know that some people wear themselves out trying to fulfil a vision God did not give them just to win or demonstrate that they are as talented as their peers, brother, sister and sometimes their parents.

When we look at Abraham's life, he had to learn a hard lesson when God promised him a son. He was so impatient with God and worried about getting old. He took a bad decision following bad advice and ended up fathering Ishmael. As my Bishop always says, "Bad choices always lead to bad decisions; the choices you make in life are either making you or breaking you." Abraham had to live with the outcome of his decision for the rest of his life.

Furthermore, people who make these mistakes end up with the sense of failure and frustration because they are constantly measuring themselves by somebody else's assignment. It is very important that each and every one of us identify our individual talents and gifts concerning our dreams. Remember that a man's individual gifts are what bring him before great men and open doors for him. (Proverbs 18:16) The proverb speaks of a man's gift bringing him before great men — he gains entrance into the presence of those superior to him. The president of a bank will entertain large depositors, and a senator will go golfing with you for a sizable campaign contribution.

It is clear that without a clear purpose in life, one can only be changing directions, jobs, relationships, churches, etc. hoping that each change they make will settle them. This is a pure lack of focus.

> *Nothing is as potent as a focused life.*
>
> AUTHOR UNKNOWN

The power of focus can be seen in how light works. Scientists have discovered that the rays of the sun passing through a magnifying glass, can set paper on fire. But when the light is focused even more as a laser beam, it can cut through steel. In Philippians 3:13-14, Paul made it clear that,

> Brethren, I do not count myself to have apprehended; but one thing I do, forgetting those things which are behind and reaching forward to those things which are ahead, I press toward the goal for the prize of the upward call of God in Christ Jesus.

We discover here that Paul was very obsessed with focusing on his dream by making Christ known to the world. Therefore if we want our lives to create an impact then we all need to remain focused on our dream. We need to be very disciplined to remain focused and not get distracted by winds of doctrine or the affairs of this world. Sometimes our fellow brother or sister can see something that you may be doing wrong and point it out to you. Don't get upset. Be honest and ask yourself, could they be right, then pray to God and start on your road to making changes that will make you a better person for yourself as well as for God.

"Watch, stand fast in the faith, be brave, and be strong." (1 Corinthians 16:13, NKJV) As Christians striving to live the way God wants us to, we always have to be watchful about the many sinful ways around us. We have to stand fast and resist the desire to fall into the traps that the enemy is trying to set for us.

Every day we should acknowledge to God that we need Him. When we start to act like we do not need God in our lives and that we can do everything ourselves, that's when we run into problems. The next time we are about to do something, we must acknowledge God and watch Him make our situation better.

We have to realize what our purpose is in God. Only when we do that can our lives take on a new meaning and we start to work towards the destiny that God has for us.

A pastor once said new levels bring new devils. When God wants us to move forward in His love and wants us to learn more about Him and His son Jesus Christ, the devil neither likes nor wants us to move forward, so you start to see negative situations come up.

In the pursuit of destiny, many things may catch your eye but keep your eye completely on the very purpose for your life. Focusing on your past histories or background will only hinder you from seeing the future. No matter how long and depressing the past was, just look ahead. People may be calling you by your past, family members may be remembering your bad behaviour during your childhood stages but I can guarantee you that you are more than what they think

> *Never give up, for that is just the place and time that the tide will turn.*
>
> HARRIET BEECHER STOWE

they know. Your days of tears will be over soon.

> For his anger endureth but a moment; in his favour is life: weeping may endure for a night, but joy cometh in the morning. (Psalm 30:5)

> And the work of righteousness shall be peace; and the effect of righteousness, quietness and assurance forever. (Isaiah 37:17)

> Fear not; for thou shalt not be ashamed: neither be thou confounded; for thou shalt not be put to shame: for thou shalt forget the shame of thy youth, and shalt not remember the reproach of thy widowhood any more. (Isaiah 54:4)

I want to assure you that any form of reproach or anything: be they rejection, regrets, disappointments, failures which cause you to weep, the Lord God is contending on your behalf and you should hold your peace in Jesus' name. The Lord is saying to you right now that you are his battle axe and weapon of war: for with you will He break in pieces the nations, and with you he will destroy kingdoms (Jeremiah 51:20). Just remain focused in Jesus' name.

No matter where you have been, no matter where you are at this moment, if you have not found God's plan for your life; please stop what you are doing and start looking for it and begin where you are right now. God is ready to put your life back on track. He is ready to give you a sense of hope.

> For I know the thoughts that I think toward you, saith the LORD, thoughts of peace, and not of evil, to give you an expected end. (Jeremiah 29:11)

It is only a God-given hope that can sustain us through difficult and trying times. You may be wondering in your mind, 'Am I ever going to get to my destiny? Why have I not married yet? Why are others getting good jobs and building houses in the village and you have not even asked for the price of bricks? Well the good news is that God is preparing you for something great. The word of God says that "Though it tarry, wait for it, for it will surely come, and will not tarry." (Habakkuk 2:3)

We need to understand that everything has its moment and cycle: some in an hour and others in a century; but the very purpose of that particular thing (dream, plan, education, and childbirth) shall surely complete its cycle whether long or short. God's purposes and plans for your life will not be cut off but they will surely come to pass.

Brethren, instead of focusing on our problems, it is very important that we look to our God and trust His word. The Bible encourages us that,

> Many are the afflictions of the righteous: but the Lord delivereth him out of them all. (Psalm 34:19)

And also Isaiah 43:2 says,

> When thou passest through the waters, I will be with thee; and through the rivers, they shall not overflow thee: when thou walkest through the fire, thou shalt not be burned; neither shall the flame kindle upon thee.

There is hope for you and will bud, and bring forth boughs like a plant. (Job 14:9)

Above all things please do not despise or lose your precious dreams and purpose only to seek it diligently with tears.

> *If you stay focused and right on track, you will get to where you want to be.*
>
> AUTHOR UNKNOWN

Wilma Rudolph knows what she is talking about when she says, "Never underestimate the power of dreams and the influence of the human spirit," — she was the first American woman runner to win three gold medals at a single Olympics Meet.

Below are 10 key reasons why you need to ignite the power of your creative mind to create your desired future.

1. The future is created by knowledge, not ignorance. It is created through application of adequate, relevant knowledge, wisdom and understanding, not negligence.
2. The future is created by those who build with generations in mind.
3. The future is created by those who have taken the bricks thrown at them to lay a solid foundation for the release and fulfilment of their destiny.

4. The future is created by those whose lives are not lived just to conform but to transform, add value and revolutionise.

5. The future is purely determined by your daily choices and decision.

6. Your future is created by the schedule you keep daily, be it positive or negative.

7. The future is created by those who focus on the stars even though they might be in the gutter.

8. The future is created by chasing your purpose in life and not counting or relying on your pension.

9. The future is created by total dependency on God's word (Joshua 1:8).

10. The future is created by those who see great treasures in trash knowing that God is all they need to have all their needs met.

Conclusion

The secret of your future lies in igniting your creative mind. You are what you are by what you think. Therefore what you think about yourself today regarding your talents and gift will either bring you before great men or mere men.

Until you discover yourself, renew your mind, use that God given talent to add value to your generation, you have not lived to the glory and purpose of God.

God has given each and every one of us the talents and gifts; do not be like the servant who did not use his talent but buried it until his master came asking him about the profits of his talent. Your promotion, provision and your protection lie in the talent you use to add value to mankind.

When your mind is ignited and directed and is working toward a specific goal in life with the word of God, your future is guaranteed. Washington Irving observes that, "Little minds are tamed and subdued by misfortune, but great minds rise above them."

There is power in your creative mind to create your desired future only if you ignite it. As you begin to ignite the power of your creative mind, may God himself empower you to change the world as you think like the way God thinks. Be blessed.

References

Abioye David O.
- *Productive Thinking*
- *Overcoming Stagnation*

Dragos Roua, *100 Ways to Improve Your Life*

Hampel Bishop Prince, *Dreams: Direction Destiny Crossing the Rubicon of Life.*

Hutton-Wood Michael, (Bishop, Dr.)
- *Leadership Capsules*
- *I Shall Rise Again*
- *How to Negotiate Your Desired Future with Today's Currency*
- *You Need to Do the Ridiculous to Experience the Miraculous*
- *175 Reasons Why You Cannot Fail*

Maxwell John, *Developing the Leadership Within You*

Newman Bill, *The Power of Successful Life*

Oyedepo David
- *Understanding Vision*
- *In Pursuit of Vision*

Rayan Jemima, *Become a Winner*

Rhonda Jones, *You Must Change Your Mind to Change Your Life*

Staples Walter, *How to Think Like a Winner*

Whelchel Mary, *Defeating Discouragement*

BOOKS AND LEADERSHIP MANUALS
BY BISHOP MICHAEL HUTTON-WOOD

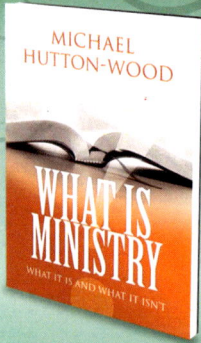

What is Ministry

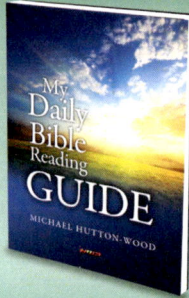

My Daily Bible
Reading Guide

Leadership Nuggets

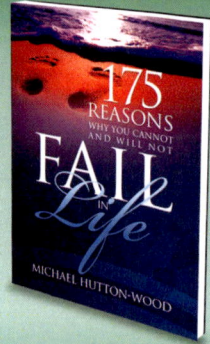

175 Reasons Why You Canno
And Will Not Fail In Life

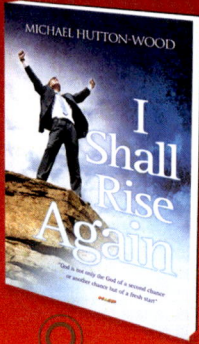

I Shall Rise Agian

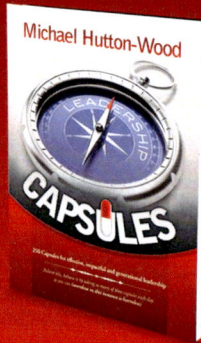

Leadership Capsules

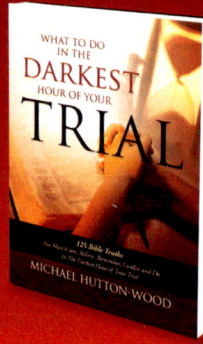

What To Do In The Darkest
Hour of Your Trial

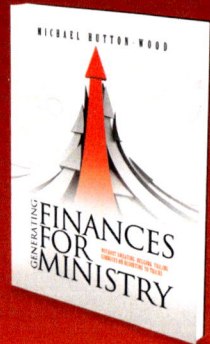

Generating Finances
For Ministry

TRAINING MANUALS FOR IMPACTFUL LEADERSHIP & EFFECTIVE MINISTRY

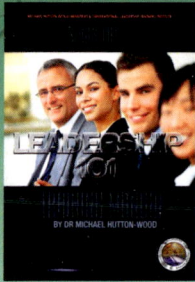

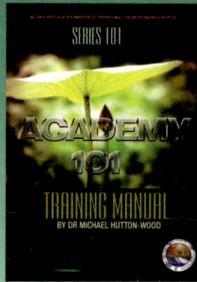

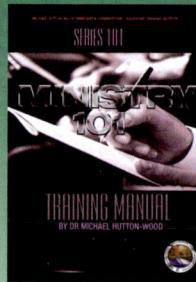

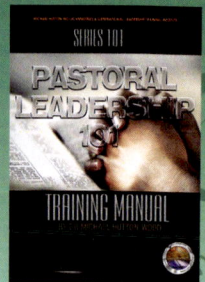

Please log on to **www.houseofjudah.org.uk** for more information